For Bobbie

All about Arthur

Eric Carle

All about Arthur
(an absolutely absurd ape)

Franklin Watts, Inc.
New York, N.Y. 1974

Library of Congress Cataloging in Publication Data

Carle, Eric.
   All about Arthur (an absolutely absurd ape)
   SUMMARY: To cure his loneliness, Arthur the ape travels from
city to city meeting other animals.
   [1. Alphabet books. 2. Animals—Stories] I. Title.
PZ10.3.C1896Al   [E]   73-9571
ISBN 0-531-02662-0

Printed in Germany.

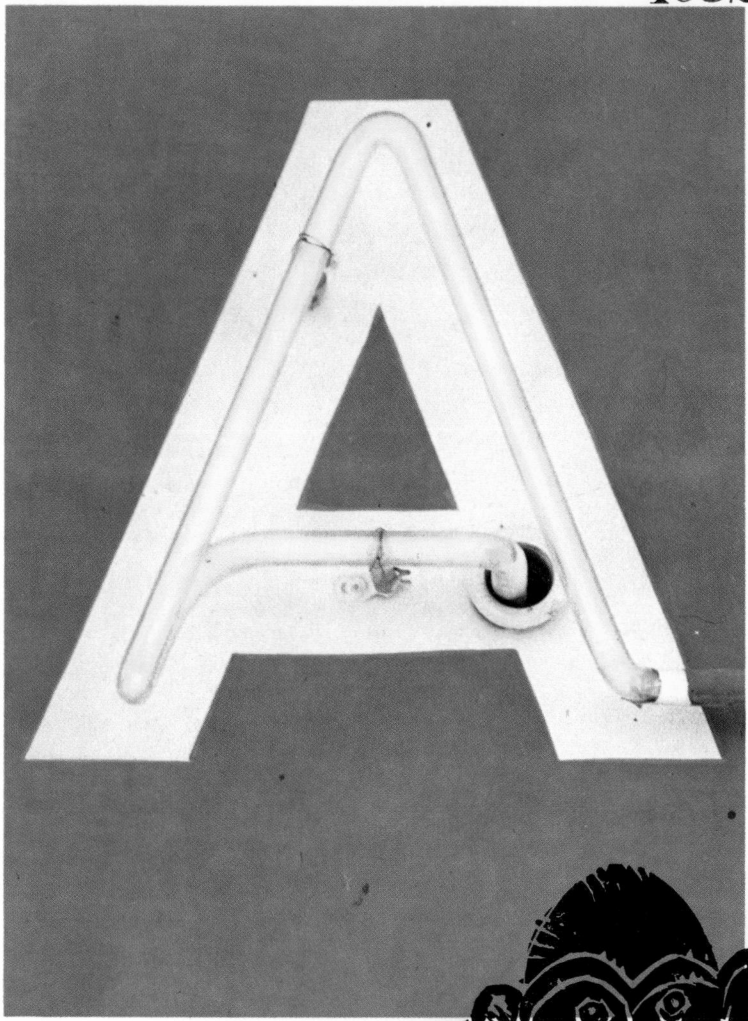

In Atlanta one autumn day
an absolutely absurd
accordion-playing ape named
Arthur felt all alone.

In Baltimore Arthur befriended a bashful banjo-playing bear named Ben. Ben was bored beyond belief.

In Cincinnati he came across a cool
calico cat selling cotton candy on a corner.
The cat was called Cindy.

In Denver down by a
dingy drugstore he met
a dapper dancing dalmatian dog
named Danny.

In Evansville by an enormous elm tree he met an eccentric but exceptionally easygoing elephant named Eddie. With Eddie was an elegant electric eel.

In Fairbanks he found four faithful friends:
a freaky frog, Fred;
a funny fish, Flora;
a frisky falcon, Fletcher;
and a fresh fox, Fay.
They called themselves "The Four Fantastics."

In Galveston he got to meet
a grumpy gazelle, Gus.
Gus was good in gymnastics
and was glad to go with
the groovy group.

In Houston on Halloween
he met haughty Harriet
and her henpecked husband Hector,
two hungry but happy hippos.

In an inn in Indiana
he met an intelligent ibex named Ivan
and an inquisitive iguana, Isabel.
Both had an interesting idea:
Let's imitate Indians.

In Jacksonville, he met a jaguar
who could juggle. His name was John.
A jolly judge had just released John
from jail.

In Kansas City he met a kind kangaroo named Kenneth who had just knocked over a kettle while kissing his kooky wife, Kate.

In Louisville he met Leo, a lonely lion
licking a lollipop; Lana, a lovely llama;
and Lisa, a little lady lizard.

At midnight he arrived in Memphis.
Under the moon he met a magnificent
mouse named Max who was a magician.
He could turn a mole into a marshmallow.

Near New York he met a nutty nightingale
wearing a necktie. His name was Nathan.

In Oklahoma he met an odd octopus
named Otto, who was eating oysters with onions.

In Philadelphia he found quite a pair
playing poker — Peter a pompous parrot,
and Quincy a quaint-looking quail.
They were quietly quarreling over a quarter.
"Pardon me," said the parrot.
"I quit!" said the quail.

In Reno on a rugged ranch
he met a rich and respectable rhino
who couldn't remember his own name!
(It was Richard.)

South of Seattle he met a
silly seal Sally suffering from the sun.
She had a scorched stomach.

In Tucson he met two troublesome
twin toucans. She was Trudy, he Theodore.
He played the trumpet, she tennis.

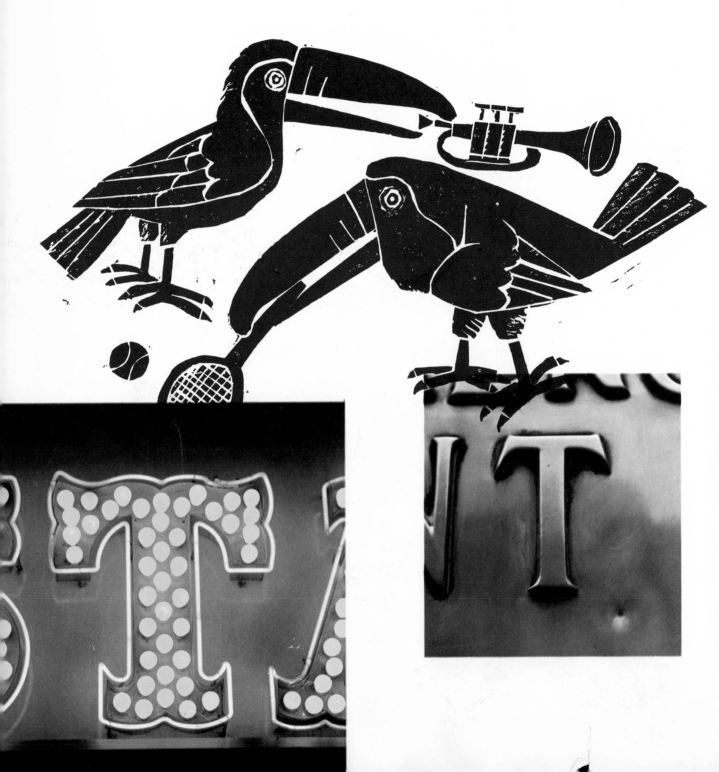

In Utica he met a unique unicorn named Uris. He was utterly useless unless he was upstairs playing the ukulele.

On a vacant lot
in Valley Forge
he met a very vain
vulture named Victoria,
sitting on a vase
viewing the valley.

In Washington, he met a wonderful walrus with whiskers. William was his name. He was worried about his weight.

In Yonkers he met Mr. X,
a zany young yak who played the
zither, the xylophone and a yo-yo
(all at the same time!).

Now Arthur doesn't feel alone anymore.

About the author

Born in the United States, Eric Carle was brought up in Germany where he studied at the Akademie der bildenden Künste in Stuttgart. He is the author/artist of several picture books, among them THE VERY HUNGRY CATERPILLAR, THE ROOSTER WHO SET OUT TO SEE THE WORLD and HAVE YOU SEEN MY CAT? He has also drawn a set of ecology posters called ERIC CARLE'S VANISHING WILD ANIMAL COUNTING POSTERS.

    Mr. Carle now lives in New York City, but his books are translated into many languages and enjoyed by children throughout the world.